AF394655

FROM WITNESS TO COMPASSION

The Stations of the Cross

Kevin Parkes

SLG Press

SLG Pocket Books 2

ISBN 978-0-7283-0509-0
SLG pocket books ISSN 2978-8633 (Print)
SLG pocket books ISSN 2978-8641 (eBooks)

Edited and typeset in Bembo Std 12 pt by Julia Craig-McFeely

Biblical quotations are taken from the New Revised Standard Version of the Bible unless otherwise noted.

Cover image: Jean-Bernard Lalanne, 'Sainte Véronique regardant la foule hostile' 2024.

SLG Press
Convent of the Incarnation
Fairacres • Oxford
www.slgpress.co.uk

Printed by
Grosvenor Group Ltd, Loughton, Essex
SLG Press Publications are printed on FSC Certified sustainable papers.

CONTENTS

FROM
WITNESS
TO
COMPASSION

Introduction

The way of the Cross is not a journey we take only through memory or imagination. It is a road that winds through the living world—through our city streets and refugee camps, through hospitals and prisons, through the quiet grief of homes where loss is present every day.

To walk this way with Christ is to recognize that his suffering is not an ancient tragedy, but a present mystery: unfolding still in those who are forgotten, displaced, exploited, or afraid.

Here, we do not come to admire endurance or pity the victim. We come to see and to be seen by the One who has entered fully into the world's pain, who bears its weight from within, and who does not turn away. Each station marks not only a step in his passion, but a revelation of the hidden life of God: a God found not above power, but beneath it; not beyond injustice, but among its casualties; not outside death, but through it into resurrection.

This devotion is not an escape from the world's suffering; it is a way of learning how to remain in it faithfully. We trace the pattern of Christ's descent so that our hearts might be shaped by his mercy: to stand where he stands, to notice what he notices, to love where he loves. Each reflection, each silence, each question invites us to hold together the sorrow and the hope of all creation, to allow compassion to take flesh again in us.

Although written for personal contemplation, this book is also suitable for use within the framework of a congregational service of the Stations of the Cross. The traditional pattern of the service begins with a short prayer and response:

We adore you, O Christ, and we bless you.
Because by your holy Cross you have redeemed the world.

Followed by the reading from Scripture, meditation and prayer. A verse of a hymn, a simple chant, or a fragment of psalmody may be sung between stations, allowing time for physical movement from one station to another.

The texts should be read slowly, to leave space for silence, and to let the rhythm of scripture and prayer draw the heart into a deeper awareness of God's presence in suffering and in love. The words seek to open us to the compassion of Christ that still takes flesh in our world.

May these meditations open our eyes to Christ's presence among the many crucified of our age—the poor, the persecuted, the displaced, the despised—and may we find in his wounded hands the promise that no suffering is ever forgotten, no death ever final, no life ever lost beyond the reach of love.

Let us walk this way together: slowly, honestly, prayerfully until, in the shadow of the Cross, we glimpse the first light of resurrection.

I

Jesus is Condemned to Death

He was despised and rejected by others; a man of suffering and acquainted with infirmity.   *Isaiah 53:3*

REFLECTION

The verdict has already been spoken, long before any words were uttered in court. The machinery of power, cold, methodical and sure of itself, grinds forward, impervious to the fragility of truth. It is a system that feeds upon its own momentum: deaf to conscience and blind to compassion.

And there, in the midst of its relentless turning, stands Jesus. Word made flesh, now rendered voiceless. The innocent one who bears the full weight of a world that finds it easier to destroy than to listen, easier to sacrifice than to face the discomfort of its own corruption. He stands where countless others have stood and still stand: before tribunals of fear, beneath the gaze of convenience, in the shadow of authority that will not be questioned.

In this moment, every unjust trial is gathered up: the silenced dissident, the exiled stranger, the prisoner without name or defence. Each finds in Jesus their reflection, their companion in suffering. His stillness becomes their witness; his silence, their protest.

We remember those judged not for what they have done but for who they are: the ones marked by the colour of their skin, by the poverty of their circumstance, by the accent that betrays their origin. The ones condemned so that society may preserve its illusion of innocence, so that the privileged need not face the pain of repentance.

Here, before this silent figure, we are summoned to a deeper seeing: to recognize that truth stands not with the powerful, but with the powerless; not in the judgment passed, but in the love that endures it. In the silence between accusation and sentence, God waits bearing all our violence, and still, incredibly, offering mercy.

PRAYER

God of justice, open our eyes to those condemned by systems that serve only fear. Give us courage to speak when truth is trampled and hearts restless until mercy prevails. Through Christ who was judged unjustly, yet forgave his accusers. Amen.

SELF–EXAMINATION

Where in the world today do I hear the cry 'Crucify' and how am I being called to stand beside the one being silenced?

II
Jesus Takes Up His Cross

Abraham took the wood of the burnt-offering and laid
it on his son Isaac.   *Genesis 22:6*

REFLECTION

The Cross is laid upon his shoulders—brutal, unre-
lenting, inevitable. He does not resist. He simply accepts what is given, though it has no justice, no reason,
no mercy. And in that acceptance, a strange reversal
begins. The sign of human cruelty becomes the gesture of Divine Love.

So many today know that same unchosen burden. The
homeless who carry the memory of home in tatters; the
carer whose arms ache with sleepless compassion; the
worker bowed by debt; the one who bears the slow,
grinding weight of mental illness. None of these crosses
are self-selected, yet all of them are carried.

In taking up the Cross, Jesus enters that hidden fellowship: the fellowship of those who endure without
applause, who keep faith in the shadows, who continue
to love when life has stripped them of choice. His
carrying gives meaning to theirs.

The world teaches us to evade the heavy things, to stay light, unencumbered, detached. But love does not travel that way. Love stoops down, stoops low enough to lift what others drop. Christ's strength is not in the avoidance of pain, but in the tenderness that refuses to abandon those who suffer.

And so the Cross, the object of shame, becomes a new language of compassion. To carry the Cross is to believe that no weight, however cruel, can silence the work of saving love that God accomplishes through endurance, solidarity, and mercy.

PRAYER

Christ our burden-bearer, walk beside all who are pressed down by injustice. Strengthen those who carry hidden crosses of loss, grief, trauma, or responsibility. Make our hands ready to lift the weight others are forced to bear, that your love may lighten their path. Amen.

SELF-EXAMINATION

Whose burden lies within my reach, waiting to be shared, if only I would stoop low enough to lift it?

III
Jesus Falls the First Time

Surely he has borne our infirmities and carried our diseases; yet we accounted him stricken, struck down by God, and afflicted. But he was wounded for our transgressions, crushed for our iniquities; upon him was the punishment that made us whole, and by his bruises we are healed.
Isaiah 53:4–5

REFLECTION

He falls—hard, graceless, unguarded. Dust rises around him, and the crowd shifts uneasily. The one they called Messiah lies broken before their feet. There is no miracle to rescue him, no sudden strength to dazzle the watchers. Only the weight of human weakness, the weight that will not be evaded.

In this first fall, we meet a God who refuses to stand above the world's failure. He enters it. The divine stoops to the dirt, breath mingling with our own. Every collapse, every exhaustion, every moment when the spirit buckles under its burden, these are now holy ground.

This is where God begins again: among those who cannot keep going but somehow do. The single parent who breaks down behind a closed door; the rough sleeper on the streets; the child waking to another day of hunger. In their fall, Christ is already kneeling.

To fall is not to fail. To fall is to find ourselves where God already waits, beneath the pretence of strength, beneath the mask of control. Love meets us there, not to erase our weakness, but to sanctify it.

In this first fall, the story of resurrection quietly stirs. For from the dust, grace always rises.

PRAYER

God of mercy, lift us when we fall beneath the weight of our own weakness. Give us compassion to kneel beside those who stumble, and the grace to know that your strength begins where ours ends.
Amen.

SELF–EXAMINATION

What part of my life have I hidden, believing it too fallen for God to enter?

IV
Jesus Meets His Mother

And a sword will pierce your own soul too. *Luke 2:35*

Their eyes meet, and the world stops. No sound but the slow grinding of the soldiers' boots, no words that can bridge this chasm of love and sorrow. The mother and the son, each beholding what cannot be borne, each holding the other with the only thing left: presence.

This is love stripped of every illusion. Mary cannot save him; Jesus cannot spare her. They meet in the terrible honesty of helplessness, where love has no power except to endure. And yet that endurance is divine. For in her steadfast gaze, God learns what it is to be human; and in his pain, humanity learns what it is to be God.

So many walk this same road: those who keep vigil beside a hospital bed, the friend who hold a hand when words have run out. Love does not always fix; it sometimes simply stays.

Mary becomes for us the icon of faithful presence: the courage to look without turning away, to remain when departure would be easier. Her gaze holds the world's suffering and transforms it into prayer.

And in that shared stillness between them, something sacred takes root: the seed of resurrection, hidden in love's endurance.

PRAYER

Mother of sorrows, stay near all who grieve without comfort. Teach us to be faithful in presence, to stand in love even when words fail, and to see in every broken bond the echo of your compassion.
Amen.

SELF–EXAMINATION

When have I been called, like Mary, simply to stay— to love without fixing, to be present without power?

V

Simon of Cyrene Helps Jesus to Carry the Cross

Bear one another's burdens, and in this way you will fulfil the law of Christ. *Galatians 6:2*

REFLECTION

Simon is taken from the crowd and pressed into service, given no choice, caught in the machinery of empire that makes use of strangers. He is not a disciple, not one of the inner circle, perhaps not even aware of the drama unfolding before him. And yet, in this moment of coercion, grace finds him.

The Cross he did not choose becomes the place where heaven meets his reluctant hands. The forced companion becomes a bearer of God's saving work. So often the call to love comes not through the doors we open, but through the interruptions we resist.

Simon stands for all who are compelled into the world's suffering: the carer who works long hours because there is no other choice; the neighbour who answers a cry for help when their own life is already overfull; the refugee who, in fleeing violence, cares for the wounded of another's war. These are the unexpected disciples of compassion, drawn into the shadow of Christ's endurance.

God's grace is not limited to our willingness. It seeps through the cracks of inconvenience, through our half-hearted 'yes,' through our fatigue. Simon's story tells us that holiness often begins at the point of interruption, where our plans are broken open and mercy steps in.

He learns, without knowing, the rhythm of salvation: to walk behind Jesus, to bear another's burden for a little while, and to discover that this shared weight is strangely light.

PRAYER

Christ who accepts help from the unwilling, teach us to see you in the stranger pressed into service.
May our hearts discover grace in the interruptions of compassion and, in carrying the world's weight, find your presence beside us.
Amen.

SELF–EXAMINATION

When have I been drawn, unwillingly or unprepared, into another's suffering and what did grace teach me there?

VI
Veronica Wipes the Face of Jesus

Hear, O Lord, when I cry aloud;
be gracious to me and answer me! ...
Your face, Lord, do I seek.
Do not hide your face from me.   *Psalm 27:8–9*

REFLECTION

Out of the crowd steps one woman, Veronica, without power, without permission, without protection. She crosses the invisible line between safety and compassion. In her hands, only a cloth; in her heart, only courage.

What she does seems so small, a gesture against the vastness of cruelty. And yet, in the eyes of heaven, it becomes an act of revelation. The face of God, beaten and bloodied, is touched by human tenderness, and the imprint remains. In that moment, we see the truth of the Incarnation: that God's glory hides in the wounded and the weary, waiting to be recognized by love.

Every day, the world offers us the same choice—to turn away from suffering, or to reach out and touch it with compassion. Each act of mercy, however fleeting, restores a fragment of the divine image that violence tries to erase.

Veronica's gesture is not grand; it is faithful. It belongs to every quiet person who tends the sick; every advocate who speaks for the voiceless; every neighbour who knocks on a door left unopened too long. In such hidden moments, Christ's face is revealed again and again.

What the world calls futile, heaven names holy. The cloth, now marked with the image of the crucified, becomes a relic not of sentiment, but of transformation. In mercy, God leaves his likeness in the hands that dare to love.

PRAYER

Christ, imprint your face upon our hearts. Let our
kindness become your icon in a world grown cold.
Remind us that every act of compassion, however small,
etches your image upon creation anew.
Amen.

SELF-EXAMINATION

When have I glimpsed the face of Christ in an unexpected act of tenderness—given or received?

VII
Jesus Falls the Second Time

Our steps are made firm by the Lord,
when he delights in our way.
though we stumble, we shall not fall headlong,
for the Lord upholds us by the hand.

Psalm 37:23–4

REFLECTION

Again, he falls. The ground rises to meet him, and the crowd sighs with the weary contempt reserved for weakness. There is no splendour in this persistence, only the slow, aching rhythm of endurance.

The Son of God stumbles a second time, and something in us protests: Should not divinity be stronger than this? Yet here is the deeper revelation: God refuses to be strong in the way we imagine. Holiness is not the refusal to fall; it is the refusal to stay fallen.

This second collapse gathers to itself all the repetitions of human pain: the addict who relapses; the peace process that falters; the hope that fades; the promise that is broken once more. In every repetition of failure, God kneels again, undeterred, holding us in the dust until we rise together.

Grace is patient beyond our comprehension. It does not rush our healing or tire of our returning. Each fall, each recovery, becomes another rhythm of divine breathing: the inhale of mercy, the exhale of strength.

And so Jesus rises again, not to prove his power, but to show us what love looks like when it refuses despair. The world's redemption is not a single triumph, but a series of holy recoveries.

PRAYER

Christ of endurance, lift us when we fall repeatedly into fear or fatigue. Give courage to those who struggle daily against habits that destroy, and patience to all who labour for justice without seeing its fruit. Let your mercy be the ground from which we rise.
Amen.

SELF–EXAMINATION

Where in my life, or in the life of our world, am I being asked to believe that falling again does not mean failure?

VIII
Jesus Meets the Women of Jerusalem

The days are surely coming, says the Lord, when I will turn their mourning into joy. *Jeremiah 31:13*

REFLECTION

Their lament rises through the dust—honest, aching, human. The women of Jerusalem weep for what they see: the brutality of power, the shattering of goodness. Yet Jesus, even in his suffering, turns their vision outward. 'Do not weep for me,' he says, 'but for yourselves, and for your children'.

He draws their compassion beyond the immediate tragedy to the deeper wound of the world. The Cross is not an isolated horror; it is the mirror of all our violence. It reflects the destruction wrought by every system that exploits the weak; every war that sacrifices children; every silence that colludes with cruelty.

Christ's words are not a rebuke, but an invitation: let your tears become fertile. Weep not only for what is happening to me, but for what is happening to you—your humanity eroded by indifference, your capacity for tenderness dulled by fear.

18

The tears of these women are the beginning of truth. They stand for the prophets who lament environmental destruction; for the activists who grieve over refugees lost at sea; for the parents mourning children consumed by conflict or poverty. Their mourning is sacred rebellion against a world too comfortable with pain.

To weep like Jesus asks, is to love beyond sentiment: to allow sorrow to deepen into compassion and compassion into the hunger for justice.

PRAYER

Christ, turn our tears into resolve. Let our compassion become justice, our grief become care for the earth and its people. Make us faithful mourners of what is broken, and builders of what might yet be whole.
Amen.

SELF–EXAMINATION

What do my tears say about the world's pain and how might they move me toward healing rather than despair?

IX
Jesus Falls the Third Time

Out of the depths I cry to you, O Lord.   *Psalm 130:1*

Once more he falls. The body, already torn and exhausted, collapses under the relentless weight. This is not simply the weakness of flesh, it is the burden of the whole of creation groaning. Three times he falls: as if to sanctify every human breaking, every final surrender to weariness.

There comes a point when even courage feels hollow, when faith itself falters under the enormity of suffering. Here, in the dust of the third fall, we see that God has entered even that despair. There is no depth of exhaustion, no abyss of grief, which love has not already navigated.

This final collapse gathers all the hidden suffering of the earth: the stateless stranded between borders; the elderly forgotten in corridors of care; the overworked, the lonely, the voiceless. In each of them, Christ has fallen again. And each fall becomes a place where heaven touches earth.

We imagine holiness as radiant strength, but here it is something quieter, something stubborn and lowly. Holiness is the refusal to abandon the broken. It is God lying in the dust beside us, whispering not escape, but endurance.

There is no triumph here, only the steady heartbeat of love that will not cease. The Cross is still ahead, yet already the resurrection is stirring, not as victory, but as persistence. The strange insistence of grace that continues to rise where everything else has fallen silent.

PRAYER

Christ, when we can go no further, stay with us in the dust of our weariness. When our hope has failed, hold us with the quiet power of your love. Let our breaking become the place where your mercy begins.
Amen.

SELF-EXAMINATION

When have I reached the end of my strength, and found, unexpectedly, that God was already waiting there?

X

Jesus is Stripped of His Garments

They divide my clothes among themselves,
and for my clothing they cast lots. *Psalm 22:18*

REFLECTION

He stands naked before the world: stripped of dignity, of privacy, of all that shields a human being from humiliation. The hands that healed are bound; the body that blessed is exposed. In this nakedness, the world's cruelty is unveiled.

Yet something profound is revealed here: God does not turn away from our shame, but enters it. Every human being who has been mocked, violated, or made to feel less than human finds their companion here. The victim of abuse, the child shamed for their poverty, the stateless person paraded before officials—all are gathered into this moment.

Jesus stands unclothed not in defeat, but in radical solidarity. Nothing is hidden now between God and humanity, no disguise, no pretence. The Word that once clothed the universe in glory now stands bare, proclaiming that even our deepest humiliation cannot separate us from love.

The soldiers gamble for his clothing; the crowd stares. Yet heaven sees a different truth: the vulnerability of God is the doorway of redemption. We are invited to stand with those who have been stripped by life, to defend their dignity as holy ground.

In Christ's exposure, we are set free from the need to hide. The garments of self-protection fall away; what remains is truth—painful and tender.

PRAYER

Christ, stripped of all but love, clothe the despised in your mercy. Heal the wounds of humiliation and restore the dignity of all who are shamed. May we learn to stand unafraid in the truth of who we are before you.
Amen.

SELF-EXAMINATION

What coverings of pride, fear, or image must I lay aside to stand honestly before God and others?

XI
Jesus is Nailed to the Cross

They have pierced my hands and feet;
I can count all my bones.   *Psalm 22:16–17 ESV*

Iron pierces flesh. The sound of the hammer echoes through creation. It is the rhythm of violence that has sounded since Cain raised his hand against Abel.

With each blow, love answers hatred not with revenge, but with forgiveness. 'Father, forgive them.' The words move through pain like light through a shattered window. The hands that stretched bread across a table are now stretched in agony, yet still they bless.

This is the still point of history: the moment when human cruelty meets divine mercy, and mercy does not turn away. The nailed Christ is not simply a victim; he is the revelation of a love that endures even the nails.

Here all the world's violence is gathered: the drone strike, the lynching, the domestic blow, the subtle cruelty of exclusion. Each nail driven into the innocent becomes an indictment and also an invitation. If love can still speak forgiveness from such pain, then there is no wound beyond healing, no hatred beyond transformation.

The Cross, once a symbol of empire's power, becomes the throne of compassion. The open arms of Christ are wide enough to hold all who suffer and even those who cause suffering.

PRAYER

Christ, nailed and forgiving, break our addiction to cruelty and vengeance. Stretch our hearts wide enough to contain even our enemies. Teach us that the power of love is stronger than the power of fear.
Amen.

SELF-EXAMINATION

Who or what in my life most needs to hear the words, 'Father, forgive them'?

XII
Jesus Dies on the Cross

It is the Passover of the Lord … The blood shall be a sign for you on the houses where you live.

Exodus 12:11, 13

REFLECTION

Darkness falls. The cry tears through the air: raw, bewildered, utterly human. 'My God, my God, why have you forsaken me?' In this moment, the mystery of the Incarnation reaches its furthest depth: God experiences God's own absence. The Word that spoke creation into being now speaks only silence.

This is not resignation; it is communion with the desolate. Here, Christ enters the loneliness of the bereaved; the despair of the suicidal; the silence of the refugee who has lost all language of belonging. Nothing is left outside the reach of divine compassion.

As his breath leaves his body, love holds steady. The world believes it has triumphed—another rebel silenced, another ideal extinguished. Yet in the tearing of the temple veil, heaven declares otherwise: what separated God and humanity has been undone. The way into the heart of mercy stands open.

Christ's death is not an escape from pain, but the transformation of it. In dying, he fills even death with God's presence. From now on, no one dies alone.

Love has gone to the end and beyond the end. The silence that follows is not emptiness, but waiting: the pause before creation begins again.

PRAYER

Christ, dying, you make death holy. Be with us at
the hour of our ending, and with all who pass
through the shadow of death today. May your Cross
become for us the tree of life.
Amen.

SELF–EXAMINATION

What fears or griefs do I need to place into the silence of Christ's final breath, trusting that love will hold them there?

XIII

Jesus is Taken Down from the Cross

They shall mourn for him, as one mourns for an only child.   *Zechariah 12:10*

REFLECTION

The crowd has gone home. The soldiers have turned away. Evening settles, silent and terrible, over the hill of execution. The body of love now hangs in stillness—limp, scarred, silent. And into that silence, hands approach. Not the hands of apostles, but those of Joseph, Nicodemus, and the women. Hands that move with reverence, trembling but unafraid.

They lower him gently, as one might lift a sleeping child. The body of God once radiant with laughter, now heavy with death, is received into the arms of those who will not abandon love, even when it lies cold.

In their careful tenderness, something profound unfolds: the world's violence gives way to reverence. Every act of care for the dead, every burial for the forgotten, every quiet tending of the lost and the poor continues this gesture of holy defiance. Love refuses to end at death.

28

The work of the Cross does not conclude with the final breath; it moves into this moment of human gentleness, where the infinite mercy of God is mirrored in the simplest act of care.

This is the beginning of resurrection, though no one yet perceives it: love honouring the broken body, love daring to touch what others fear.

We remember all those who handle the world's brokenness: the hospice nurse sitting through the small hours beside the dying; the aid worker cradling a child pulled from the sea; the paramedic who pauses in silence after the siren stops; the neighbour who offers help to the stranger. Each, knowingly or not, takes Christ from the Cross and lays him in their arms.

PRAYER

Christ, giver of reverence, teach us to handle every human body with honour—the living, the dying, the dead. Let love be the final word we speak over every life. Amen.

SELF-EXAMINATION

When have I been invited to treat what seemed lifeless or hopeless with tenderness and discovered holiness in the act?

XIV
Jesus is Laid in the Tomb

Unless a grain of wheat falls into the earth and dies,
it remains just a single grain; but if it dies, it bears
much fruit.   *John 12:24*

REFLECTION

The stone rolls into place. Darkness encloses the body.
All that could be done has been done. The women
linger at the threshold, unwilling to leave, uncertain of
what faith can mean when hope is buried.

The tomb is not merely a resting place; it is the deep
silence into which God descends. This is the Sabbath
of creation—the long pause between endings and be-
ginnings, when nothing seems to move and yet everything is being remade.

In that silence, the buried seed of love lies hidden,
gathering the power of a new dawn. Resurrection is
already gestating in the shadows. But for now, the
world waits.

We too know such tombs: the closed doors of grief;
the sealed rooms of depression; the hopeless corridors
of poverty and exile. We know the weight of the stone

that says, 'It is finished,' when in truth, something un-
seen is just beginning.

Faith, in this darkness, is not the denial of despair, but
its transformation. To wait with Christ in the tomb is
to trust that God's work continues even when all signs
of life have gone.

The women keep vigil outside, love refusing to
abandon what death claims. Their waiting becomes the
first prayer of Easter—the prayer of those who hope
without proof, who believe without light.

PRAYER

Christ of the hidden day, teach us to wait when hope is
buried. Keep faith alive in our darkness and prepare us
for the dawn of your rising.
Amen.

SELF–EXAMINATION

**What tomb, personal or communal, am I being
called to wait beside, trusting that even here, God
is at work?**

Living the Way of the Cross

The journey does not end at the tomb. It continues, quietly and persistently, in every place where love must choose to endure. We walk away from these stations not as spectators of an ancient sorrow, but as those who have glimpsed the pattern of Christ woven through our own life.

The Way of the Cross is not confined to church or prayer. It unfolds in the long corridors of hospitals, in the restless ache of forgiveness, in the courage of those who speak truth at cost. It is traced in the faces of neighbours and strangers, in the hands that lift, tend, feed, and bless.

To live the Stations is to see differently: to recognize that each encounter carries the possibility of God's saving work; that each human being bears the weight and the wonder of the divine image. We meet the condemned in the wronged and forgotten; we shoulder the Cross in the burdens we share; we fall and rise again in the rhythm of our own failures and forgiveness.

If we have prayed these stations well, they will not leave us unchanged. They will work like leaven in the heart: softening judgment, deepening compassion, teaching us to pause before one another's pain. They will remind us that resurrection begins not in triumph, but in faithfulness; not in the absence of suffering, but in the steadfastness of love.

May we walk on this way not once a year, but each day: learning to find Christ where the world would least expect him; learning to love where hope seems most hidden; and learning, finally, that every road if walked in mercy, becomes a way of the Cross and a way toward new life.

Final Prayer

Prayer of Surrender

Abba, Father,
I abandon myself into your hands;
do with me what you will.

Whatever you may do, I thank you;
I am ready for all, I accept all.

Let only your will be done in me,
and in all your creatures;
I wish no more than this, O Lord.

Into your hands I commend my spirit;
I offer it to you
with all the love of my heart,
for I love you, Lord,
and so need to give myself,
to surrender myself into your hands,
without reserve,
and with boundless confidence,
for you are my Father.

CHARLES DE FOUCAULD

SLG PRESS PUBLICATIONS

SLG Pocket Books

The Reconcilers, Sister Isabel SLG
From Witness to Compassion, Kevin Parkes

Fairacres Publications

Prayer and the Life of Reconciliation, Gilbert Shaw
Aloneness not Loneliness, Mother Mary Clare SLG
Intercession, Mother Mary Clare SLG
Prayer: Extracts from the Teaching of Father Gilbert Shaw, Gilbert Shaw
Learning to Pray, Mother Mary Clare SLG
Death, the Gateway to Life, Gilbert Shaw
The Victory of the Cross, Dumitru Stăniloae
The Message of Saint Seraphim, Irina Gorainov
Julian of Norwich: Four Studies to Commemorate the Sixth Centenary of the Revelations of Divine Love, Sister Benedicta Ward SLG, Sister Eileen Mary SLG, Sister Mary Paul SLG, A. M. Allchin
The Power of the Name: The Jesus Prayer in Orthodox Spirituality, Kallistos Ware
Prayer and Contemplation and Distractions are for Healing, Robert Llewelyn
The Wisdom of the Desert Fathers, trans. Sister Benedicta Ward SLG
Letters of Saint Antony the Great, trans. Derwas Chitty
From Loneliness to Solitude, Roland Walls
Theology and Spirituality, Andrew Louth
Kabir: The Way of Love and Paradox, Sister Rosemary SLG
Anselm of Canterbury: A Monastic Scholar, Sister Benedicta Ward SLG
Mary and the Mystery of the Incarnation: An Essay on the Mother of God in the Theology of Karl Barth, Andrew Louth
Trinity and Incarnation in Anglican Tradition, A. M. Allchin
Facing Depression, Gonville ffrench-Beytagh
The Single Person, Philip Welsh
The Letters of Ammonas, Successor of St Antony, trans. Derwas Chitty, introd. Sebastian Brock
George Herbert, Priest and Poet, Kenneth Mason
A Study of Wisdom: Three Tracts by the Author of The Cloud of Unknowing, trans. Clifton Wolters

Ann Griffiths and Her Writings, Llewellyn Cumings
The Our Father, Sister Benedicta Ward SLG
The Spiritual Wisdom of the Syriac Book of Steps, Robert A. Kitchen
The Prayer of Silence, Alexander Ryrie
On Tour in Byzantium: Excerpts from The Spiritual Meadow of John Moschus, Ralph Martin SSM
Monastic Life, Bonnie Thurston
Shall All Be Well? Reflections for Holy Week, Graham Ward
Solitude and Communion: Papers on the Hermit Life, ed. A. M. Allchin
The Prayers of Jacob of Serugh, ed. Mary Hansbury
The Monastic Hours of Prayer, Sister Benedicta Ward SLG
The Desert of the Heart: Daily Readings with the Desert Fathers, trans. Sister Benedicta Ward SLG
In Company with Christ: Lent, Palm Sunday, Good Friday & Easter to Pentecost, Sister Benedicta Ward SLG
Lazarus: Come Out! Reflections on John 11, Bonnie Thurston
Unknowing & Astonishment: Meditations on Faith for the Long Haul, Christopher Scott
Pondering, Praying, Preaching: Romans 8, Bonnie Thurston
Shem`on the Graceful: Discourse on the Solitary Life, trans. and introd. Mary Hansbury
God Under My Roof: Celtic Songs and Blessings, Esther de Waal
Journeying with the Jesus Prayer, James F. Wellington
Poet of the Word: Re-reading Scripture with Ephraem the Syrian, Aelred Partridge OC
Identity and Ritual, Alan Griffiths
River of the Spirit: The Spirituality of Simon Barrington-Ward, Andy Lord
Prayer and the Struggle against Evil, John Barton, Daniel Lloyd, James Ramsay, Alexander Ryrie
Dante's Spiritual Journey: A Reading of the Divine Comedy, Tony Dickinson
Jesus the Undistorted Image of God, John Townroe
Our Deepest Desire: Prayer, Fasting & Almsgiving in the Writings of Saint Augustine of Hippo, Sister Susan SLG
Lent with George Herbert, Tony Dickinson
Four Ways to the Cross, Tony Dickinson
Anselm of Canterbury, Teacher of Prayer, Sister Benedicta Ward SLG
With One Heart and Mind: Prayers out of Stillness, Anthony Kemp
Sayings of the Urban Fathers & Mothers, James Ashdown
Doors, Sister Raphael SLG
Monastic Vocation, Sisters of the Love of God, Bishop Rowan Williams

An Ecology of the Heart: Faith Through the Climate Crisis, Duncan Forbes
'In the image of the Image': Gregory of Nyssa's Opposition to Slavery,
    Adam Couchman
Gregory of Nyssa and the Sins of Asia Minor, Jonathan Farrugia
Discovery, Arthur Bell
Living Healing: The Spirituality of Leanne Payne, Andy Lord
Still Listening: Sowing the Seeds of the Jesus Prayer, Bruce Batstone CJN
*Julian of Norwich: Four Essays to Commemorate 650 Years of the Revelations of
    Divine Love*, Bishop Graham Usher, Father Colin CSWG, Sister
    Elizabeth Ruth Obbard OC, Mother Hilary Crupi OJN
TIME, Dumitru Stăniloae, Kallistos Ware
Pearls of Life: A Lifebelt for the Spirit, Tony Dickinson
The Way and the Truth and the Life: An Exploration by a Follower of the Way,
    James Ramsay
Cosmos, Crisis & Christ: Essays of Wendy Robinson, Wendy Robinson
Towards a Theology of Psychotherapy: The Spirituality of Wendy Robinson,
    Andrew Louth
Immersed in God and the World: Living Priestly Ministry, Andy Lord
The Road to Emmaus: A Sculptor's Journey through Time, Rodney Munday
Prayer Too Deep for Words, Sister Edmée SLG
The Prayers of St Isaac of Nineveh, Sebastian Brock
Two Medieval English Saints: Cuthbert and Alban, Sister Benedicta Ward SLG
Encountering the Depths, Mother Mary Clare SLG
Conflict and Concord, Sister Susan SLG, Bishop Humphrey Southern,
    Bronwen Neil, Sister Rosemary SLG, Sister Clare-Louise SLG
Divine Love in the Song of Songs, Sister Edmée SLG
Zeal for the Faith: An Introduction to Christian-Muslim Dialogue, Tony Dickinson
Bernard & Abelard, Sister Edmée SLG
*Eliot's Transitions: T. S. Eliot's Search for Identity and the Society of the Sacred
    Mission at Kelham Hall*, Vincent Strudwick
Landscape, Soul and Spirit: Ecology, Prayer and Robert Macfarlane, Andy Lord
Our Home is in God, John Townroe
Signs of the Times: A Brief Survey of the Bible's Apocalyptic Writings,
    Tony Dickinson
And We Shall be Changed: Christian Reflections on Death and Dying,
    James Ramsay
Journeys into the Bible, Sister Edmée SLG
Directions, Sister Edmée SLG
Loving Yourself, Richard Frost
Angels, Sister Raphael SLG

Contemplative Church: Pondering Church in Challenging Times, Andy Lord
Stations of the Cross, Donald McChesney, Jean-Bernard Lalanne
Being Christian among Britain's Muslims, Nicholas Heale
Create in me a Clean Heart, James Coutts
Instruments of the Passion, Lucy McKitterick
People with Dementia as Teachers of Faith, Regina Schlingheider
Faces in the Crowd, Tony Dickinson

www.slgpress.co.uk